CHILDREN'S FAVOURITE
BIBLE STORIES
from the
Old Testament

Based on stories by Patricia Hunt

Illustrated by Angus McBride

Ward Lock Limited · London

© Text Patricia Hunt 1981, 1984
© Illustrations Ward Lock Ltd 1981

This edition first published in Great Britain in 1984
by Ward Lock Limited, 82 Gower Street,
London WC1E 6EQ, a Pentos Company.

Filmset in Bookman by Text Filmsetters Ltd,
Orpington, Kent

Printed and bound in Italy by
Poligrafici Calderara, Bologna

British Library Cataloguing in Publication Data

Hunt, Patricia
    People of the Old Testament – (Children's
    favourite Bible stories; 3)

I. Title   II. McBride, Angus   III. Series
221.9′505   BS551.2

ISBN 0-7063-6323-X

Contents

Adam and Eve

In the Garden of Eden there grew all sorts of beautiful trees, which bore good fruit. A stream flowed through the garden to water it and, beyond Eden, this divided into four rivers; they were called the Pishon, the Gihon, the Tigris, and the Euphrates.

There were also two special trees in the middle of the garden. One was the Tree of Life and the other was the Tree of the Knowledge of Good and Evil.

God put Adam in the Garden of Eden, to cultivate it and take care of it, and so be a fellow-worker with Him. He said to Adam, 'You may eat the fruit of any of the trees except the fruit from the Tree of the Knowledge of Good and Evil. That fruit you must not eat; if you do then you will surely die.'

Then God brought all the animals and birds in front of Adam, and Adam gave them all their names.

God had decided that it was not good for Adam to be alone so when Adam was asleep, He took one of Adam's ribs and from it He made a woman to share life in the garden with Adam.

Adam named her Eve, and they both began a happy life together looking after the beautiful garden and everything in it.

One of the creatures living in the garden was a snake, and he was very cunning. One day he glided up to Eve and said, 'Did God really say that you must not eat the fruit of any of the trees in the garden?'

'No,' replied Eve, 'we may eat the fruit from any of the trees, except from that tree in the middle – the tree which is called the Tree of the Knowledge of Good and Evil. God said that if we ate any of that fruit, then we would surely die.'

The crafty snake smiled a cunning smile within himself. 'That's not true, you know,' he hissed. 'God said that because He knew that if you ate that fruit, then you would know all about good and evil, and so you would be like God Himself.'

Eve looked at the beautiful tree again and saw how delicious its fruit looked. Perhaps a taste would not matter – and it would be wonderful to be as wise as God, she thought. So she plucked one of the tempting fruits and ate it. It tasted nice, so she gave some to Adam and he ate too.

However, as soon as they had eaten, they suddenly realized what they had done and both felt very ashamed that they had disobeyed God. They knew they had chosen their own way and not God's, and that they had spoilt the beauty of that perfect garden by doing wrong. For the first time they became aware that they were naked and in their embarrassment they rushed to make clothing for themselves out of leaves.

That same evening, they heard God walking in the garden, but they felt so guilty that they ran away and tried to hide from Him among the trees.

But God called out, 'Adam, where are you?'

'I heard You coming,' answered Adam, 'and I was afraid, so I hid myself from You.'

'Have you eaten any of the fruit that I commanded you not to eat?' asked God.

'Eve gave the fruit to me and I ate it,' said Adam.

God turned to Eve and said, 'Why did you do this?'

Eve said, 'The snake tricked me into it.'

God was very sad at what had happened, for he felt that Adam and Eve could no longer be trusted and He knew that their wrong-doing had to be punished.

Then He turned to the snake and said, 'You, of all the animals, must bear the punishment for this. From now on you will have to crawl along the earth and eat dust for as long as you live. You and the woman will always be enemies with one another.'

To Eve God said, 'You will have to suffer pain when your children are born.' And to Adam He said, 'You listened to your wife and you ate the fruit which I had forbidden you to eat. Because of this you will have to work hard all your life to make the earth produce enough food for you. There will always be weeds and thorns, and you will have to toil all the time to make anything grow.'

Then God said, 'Now man has become like Me and has knowledge of good and evil. He cannot be allowed to eat the fruit of the Tree of Life also and thus live forever.'

So God sent Adam and Eve out of the Garden of Eden, and Adam was set to work to cultivate the land outside it.

Cain and Abel

In due time Adam and Eve had two
sons. The one born first they named
Cain, and the one who was born next
they named Abel. When the boys
grew up, Cain became a farmer and
Abel became a shepherd.

One day they both went to make their offering to God as was the custom then, just as it is today when people still bring offerings to their church at Harvest Thanksgiving and other festivals. Cain brought some of the best crops and fruit which he had grown, and Abel brought the first lamb born to one of his sheep and gave the best parts of it.

Now God was pleased with Abel's gift, because it had been given in the right spirit; but somehow Cain had the wrong attitude to giving his, and so God was not pleased with it.

Cain became very angry that his gift was not acceptable, and he scowled in fury at his brother.

'Why are you so angry?' asked God. 'Why are you frowning like that? If you had offered your gift in the right spirit, you would be smiling now instead of looking as black as thunder. You must be careful, for it is just when you feel as you do now that sin is waiting to conquer you and make you do worse things. You must overcome it.'

But Cain didn't listen to this good advice. He just let his angry feelings smoulder inside him and, as God had warned, his thoughts soon turned into deeds.

Not long afterwards Cain said to Abel, 'Let's go out into the open country.' Abel agreed, so off they went; and when they were far out into the fields, Cain turned upon his brother and killed him.

Perhaps he thought that as they were far away from everyone, no one would ever find out what he had done; but God knew, and He asked Cain, 'Where is your brother Abel?'

Cain was scared and made things worse by replying, 'I don't know. Am I supposed to look after my brother all the time?'

He knew perfectly well that the answer to that was 'Yes', but he tried to hide his wicked deed.

'What have you done?' said God. 'Your brother's blood is crying out to me from the ground like a voice calling for revenge. You must leave here. No longer may you farm the earth which has soaked up your brother's blood. If you try to grow crops, the land will not produce anything. From now on you will remain a homeless wanderer.'

Cain was horrified. He said to God, 'This punishment is much too great for me to bear. You are driving me away from the land and from Your presence.' For Cain thought that God could only be found in his old home. He did not know that God was everywhere.

'I shall be a fugitive,' Cain went on, 'a wanderer, and anyone who finds me will kill me.'

Cain must have shown the beginnings of sorrow, for God put a special mark upon him as a warning to anyone who met him not to kill him.

Later Adam and Eve had another son named Seth, and Eve became less unhappy and said, 'God has given me a son in place of Abel whom Cain killed.'

Noah and the Flood

The sins of Adam and Eve and of Cain, their son, had brought evil into the world, and for a while people became very bad indeed and allowed their wicked thoughts to grow into deeds. God saw all the evil and violence these caused and He was sad.

However, there was one man with whom God was very pleased. He was a good man and his thoughts and deeds were noble and right. His name was Noah.

One day God said to Noah, 'I have decided that this evil on earth cannot continue. A new start must be made; therefore a great flood will come which will destroy the wicked. Build yourself a boat – an ark – out of good timber; cover it with tar both inside and out, and make rooms inside it and a roof over it. Then, when the flood comes, you and your wife, and your sons and their wives, will all be safe in the boat. Into the boat take two of every kind of living creature – birds, animals and creeping things – a male and a female of each, so that they will be able to reproduce again on the earth.'

Noah found this news rather startling, but he knew that he must do as God had said. He told his three sons, named Shem, Ham and Japheth, that they would have to help him with the building of the ark so that it would be ready in time.

When the ark was finished, Noah and his family began to round up all the animals, birds, insects and reptiles, as God had directed, and together they all went into the ark and the door was firmly closed behind them. Then they settled down to watch the weather and wait for the promised rain.

Seven days later, it began to rain; and it rained in torrents, never stopping, for forty whole days and forty whole nights. The waters rose higher and higher, and the floods covered the whole earth, drowning every living thing. There was nothing left alive in the world except Noah, his family and the animals in his keeping.

Soon the ark was way above the tops of the highest mountains and there was nothing to be seen in any direction except water.

Then a great wind began to blow, and at last the waters started to go down. The rains stopped and gradually the waters began to go lower and lower. Finally, the ark came to rest on a mountain called Ararat.

Noah wanted to know if the flood waters had gone down elsewhere, so one day he opened a window in the

ark and let a raven fly out. It flew away and did not come back.

Next Noah sent out a dove but the dove could not find anywhere to land and, after a while, it flew back to the ark.

After a week, Noah sent the dove out again. On the evening of that day it came back and, in its beak, it held a fresh olive leaf. Now Noah knew that somewhere the waters had gone down far enough for the trees to be appearing again.

In time the ground became completely dry and the waters disappeared.

Then God said to Noah, 'You may now leave the boat. Take your wife with you, and your sons and their wives, and all the birds and animals, so that they can settle on the earth and start having families again to replace all those that were drowned in the great flood. Never again will I destroy all living creatures as I have done this time. As long as there is a world, there will always be seed-time and harvest, cold and heat, summer and winter, day and night, and they shall not cease.'

Abraham

When Abram was an old man, God spoke to him and said, 'You must leave your country and your native home and go to a land which I will show to you. You will have many descendants and they will become a great nation. I will bless you, and your name will become famous.'

Abram had no idea where this new land was, but he believed and trusted in God, so he set out with his wife Sarai, his family and a great company of slaves and cattle and all their other possessions.

Finally, Abram settled in the southern part of Canaan, and God said to him, 'Look in all directions. This is the land which I am going to give you and your children and their children, and it will be yours for ever. You will have so many descendants that no one will be able to count them all.'

Although Abram had no children at that time, he believed and trusted in God's word. He set up his camp near the sacred trees of Mamre at Hebron, and there he built an altar to the Lord.

One day the voice of God spoke to him and said, 'I am the Almighty God. Obey me and always do what is right. Your name will no longer be Abram, but Abraham; no longer shall you call your wife Sarai; from now on her name is Sarah. I will bless her, and she will be the mother of many peoples, and there will be kings among her descendants.'

Abraham must have found this news hard to believe, for both he and Sarah were very old.

One hot day Abraham was sitting by the door of his tent when he looked up and saw three strangers coming towards him. Abraham offered them something to eat and drink.

He took bread, cream, milk and some tender meat and set it before his guests.

Then the visitors asked him, 'Where is your wife?'

'She is in the tent,' answered Abraham.

'In the spring, she will have a son,' said one of the men.

Sarah was just behind the tent entrance, and she heard what the man had said, and she laughed. 'I am much too old to have a baby,' she thought to herself, 'and Abraham is too old to be a father.'

'Why did Sarah laugh?' Abraham was asked. 'Is there anything which is too hard for the Lord to do?'

The strangers left and Abraham walked with them part of the way. By

now he had realized that the men were messengers from God. He knew that if God had planned it, then Sarah would certainly have a son.

The promise which the strangers had brought to Abraham from God came true, and before long Sarah had a son, just as they had said. Abraham and Sarah were delighted, and they called the boy Isaac.

'God has brought me great joy and laughter,' said Sarah.

Isaac grew up to be a fine boy and his parents loved him very much.

The Sacrifice of Isaac

When Isaac was still a young man, God put Abraham to the test to see whether he really trusted Him.

He called to him one day, 'Abraham!'

'Take your son,' said God, 'your only son, Isaac, whom you love so much, and set out for the land of Moriah. I will show you a mountain there, and on it I want you to offer your son as a sacrifice to Me.'

Abraham must have wondered if he had heard God rightly. In those days human sacrifices were not uncommon, and people always offered to God the best that they had, but could God really want Abraham to kill and offer his only son whom God Himself had sent?

However, Abraham's trust in God was very great, and he believed that God's commands must be obeyed, so he did not delay.

Early next morning he called Isaac and told him they were going off into the mountains to make a sacrifice to God.

After three days' journeying they reached the mountain and began to climb it.

Abraham carried the knife and the coals for the fire, while Isaac carried the wood. As they climbed the mountain, Isaac began to look puzzled and at last he said, 'Father, we have the coals and the wood, but where is the lamb which we are going to sacrifice?'

All Abraham could reply was, 'God Himself will provide one.' With that Isaac had to be content, and the two of them walked on together.

When they arrived at the place of which God had told him, Abraham began to build an altar and to arrange the wood on it. Then he took Isaac and bound him and placed him on the altar, on top of the wood. He stretched out his hand and took the knife to slay his son.

At that moment the voice of an angel called out to him from heaven, 'Abraham, Abraham! Do not lay your hand on the boy or do anything to hurt him. Now I know that you really trust God, because you have not kept back your only son from Him.'

What a great relief Abraham felt! He looked round and there he saw a ram with its horns caught in a bush. God had sent it for him to sacrifice. He went over and freed it, and offered it as a sacrifice in place of his son.

God was pleased with this great proof of Abraham's love and trust.

Joseph and the Coat of Many Colours

Joseph was the eleventh son of Jacob, and he was his father's favourite, which made the other brothers very jealous. When Jacob gave Joseph a beautiful, long, multi-coloured robe, with sleeves, they were even more envious, for this was the kind of coat worn by persons of distinction.

One night, when Joseph was still in his teens, he had a dream. Later he told his brothers about it.

'I dreamt we were all in the fields, tying up sheaves of wheat,' he said, 'and my sheaf stood upright while yours stood in a circle round mine and bowed down to it.'

In those days people thought that dreams were a sign of what would happen in the future, so Joseph's brothers were naturally very angry at this and said, 'Do you think you are going to be a king and reign over us then?'

Then Joseph had a second dream, which he told to his brothers and also to his father. 'This time I saw the sun and the moon and eleven stars all bowing down to me,' he said.

Jacob was not very pleased when he heard this, and he said, 'Do you mean that your mother, your

brothers and I will all bow down to you?'; but although he scolded Joseph, Jacob could not help thinking about the dream and wondering what it all meant.

One day, as Joseph's brothers tended the sheep, they began to plot against him. 'Let's kill him and throw his body into one of these pits. Then when we're asked, we can say that a wild animal has killed him. We'll see then what will become of his dreams!'

One of the brothers, named Reuben, was not very happy about this plan, and he tried to save Joseph. 'Let us not kill him' he said, 'but just throw him into the pit without hurting him — for after all, he is our brother.' Reuben hoped he might be able to rescue Joseph later on and send him back to their father unhurt.

When Joseph came the brothers ripped off his splendid robe and threw him down into the pit. Then they sat down to have their meal.

Suddenly they heard a noise and looked up to see a procession of camels approaching. They belonged to a party of Ishmaelite traders who were journeying to Egypt, and they were laden with all kinds of goods

which the traders were taking to sell.

One of the brothers, Judah, had an idea. 'What will we gain if we do kill Joseph and then have to cover up the murder?' he said. 'Let's sell him to these traders instead; then we won't be hurting our own flesh and blood.'

The brothers thought this a good idea and, when the traders came near, they hauled Joseph out of the pit and sold him to them for twenty pieces of silver.

Reuben hadn't been with them while this was happening; he was, perhaps, tending the sheep. When he came back and found Joseph gone, he was most upset. 'What shall I do?' he cried. 'The boy has gone!' But it was too late for him to do anything to save his brother.

Next, the other brothers killed a goat and dipped Joseph's robe in its blood. Then they took the coat home and showed it to their father. 'We found this,' they exclaimed. 'Does it belong to Joseph?'

'Yes, yes, it does!' cried the old man in horror. 'Some wild animal must have torn him to pieces!'

Jacob wept and mourned for Joseph for a very long time. Although his family tried in every way to comfort him, he would not be consoled for the death of his favourite son. 'I will still be mourning for Joseph when I die,' he said.

Joseph's New Life

Meanwhile the traders and Joseph had arrived in Egypt, and there he was sold to a man named Potiphar who was one of the officers of the Pharaoh, the King of Egypt, and captain of the palace guard.

So Joseph lived in the house of his new Egyptian master and, because God was with him, he was successful in all that he did.

Potiphar made him his personal servant and put him in charge of his house and all that he owned.

Potiphar's wife, however, was not so nice, and she told lies about Joseph to her husband. She said Joseph had behaved very wickedly towards her. This was completely untrue, but unfortunately Potiphar believed his wife and had Joseph thrown into prison.

Here the jailer soon realized that Joseph was indeed a trustworthy man. He put him in charge of the other prisoners, and made him responsible for all the work that was done in the prison.

Some time later two other officials were put into the prison. One was Pharaoh's butler, or cupbearer, and the other was his chief baker. Both had offended Pharaoh and they were due to spend a long time in jail.

One morning Joseph went to their cell and found them both looking very miserable. 'What's the matter with you two?' he asked. 'Why are you looking so worried?'

They answered, 'We both had a dream last night and there is no one here who can tell us what the dreams mean.'

'Only God knows the meaning of dreams,' said Joseph. 'But tell them to me and I will ask Him to help us understand them.'

So the butler said, 'In my dream I saw a grapevine with three branches on it. The leaves came out, then the blossom, and then the grapes ripened. I held Pharoah's cup under the grapes and squeezed the juice into it and gave it to him.'

'The three branches are three days,' said Joseph, 'and it means that in three days Pharaoh will set you free and restore you to your old position.

Then the chief baker told his dream. 'I was carrying three bread-baskets on my head,' he began, 'and in the top one were all kinds of baked food for Pharoah, and the birds were eating them up.'

Joseph told the baker that his dream had a sad meaning. 'It means that in three days Pharaoh will have you hanged and the birds will eat your flesh.' Three days later it was Pharaoh's birthday and he gave a party for all his officials. He released the butler and the baker, gave the butler his old job back, and had the chief baker hanged – just as Joseph had said.

Pharaoh's Dream

Pharaoh himself had a dream. He dreamt he was standing by the River Nile when seven fat cows came up out of the water and began to eat the grass. Then seven thin bony cows came up and stood by the fat cows on the riverbank; and the thin cows ate up the fat cows. And then Pharaoh woke up.

He soon fell asleep again and this time he had another dream. Now he saw seven fat, full ears of corn, all growing on one stalk; then seven more ears grew which were thin and damaged by the east wind. And the thin ears swallowed up the fat ones.

Pharaoh awoke feeling very worried. He knew it had only been a dream, but he was sure the dreams meant something. So he sent for all his magicians and courtiers and all his wise men and asked them, but none of them had any idea what the dreams meant.

Suddenly the butler remembered Joseph. At once he went to Pharaoh and said, 'Two years ago you were angry with me and put me in prison along with the chief baker. While we were there, we both had a dream, and there was a young Hebrew man, also a prisoner, who was able to tell us the meaning of our dreams. And all he told us came true!'

'Send for him,' commanded Pharaoh, and Joseph was quickly brought out of his dungeon and taken to see Pharaoh. 'I have had a dream,' said Pharaoh, 'and no one can explain it, but I have been told that when you hear a dream you can interpret it.'

'No, your Majesty,' said Joseph. 'I

can't, but God can. I can only tell you the interpretation which God gives.'

Then Pharaoh told his dreams to Joseph.

Joseph said, 'The two dreams really mean the same thing, and through them God is telling you what is going to happen. The seven fat cows are seven years, and the seven full ears of corn are seven years; the seven thin cattle and the seven poor, empty ears are also seven years. What it means is that there will be seven years of plenty – good harvests and more than enough food for everyone. These will be followed by seven years of terrible famine and poor harvests – so bad that the seven good years will be forgotten. The fact that you have had the dream twice means that the matter is fixed by God.

'I think you should appoint a wise and careful man and put him in charge of the whole country. Then appoint overseers to take a fifth part of all the produce of the land during the seven good years. The officials can store all of this up. Thus it will be at hand when the famine comes, so the people will not starve.'

Pharaoh and his servants thought this was a very good idea. The only problem was where could they find a man wise, honest and clever enough to take charge of the whole plan. Then Pharaoh thought, 'Who could be better than Joseph himself? The spirit of this god must be in him.'

He said to Joseph, 'Since your god has shown you all this, I will put you in charge of the country, and everyone must obey your orders. Only as regards the throne will I be greater than you. Your authority will be second only to mine. I will appoint you governor over all Egypt.'

Then Pharaoh took a ring from his finger and put it on to Joseph's finger. He put fine linen robes on him and a gold chain round his neck; and he gave him his second-best chariot to ride in.

Joseph was thirty years old when he began his great task as governor of Egypt, and he travelled all over the country making provision for the famine which was ahead of them.

During the seven good years the land produced huge crops of corn, and Joseph had it collected and stored in the cities.

Then the seven years of plenty came to an end, and the seven years of famine started. There was famine in other countries as well, but because of Joseph's wise plan, there was food in Egypt. When the people felt hungry and went to Pharaoh, he told them, 'Go to Joseph and do as he tells you.' And Joseph opened the storehouses and sold the corn which he had stored.

People came from all over the world to buy some of Egypt's corn, because there was such a severe shortage everywhere else.

The Baby in the Bulrushes

Some years later, after Joseph had died, a new Pharaoh came to rule over Egypt. By this time Jacob's descendants, the Israelites, had been living in Egypt for many years, and there were now a great number of them.

The new Pharaoh knew nothing about Joseph and all that he had done to save the people from starvation, and he said, 'These Israelites are getting so many that they are becoming a threat to us. If there was a war they might join up with our enemies. We must find a way to suppress them.'

So the Egyptians put slave-drivers over the Israelites to make them work harder and harder, and they made them build store-cities for Pharaoh.

Pharaoh made an order to all the people saying that every new baby boy born to the Israelites should be drowned in the River Nile, but that they could let the girls live.

Naturally the Hebrews were most unhappy about this law. One family already had two children, and to them another baby boy was born. He was a fine boy, and the mother could not bear to see him drowned, so she managed to keep him hidden for three months.

As he grew bigger, the time came when she could hide him no longer. She made a little basket from the bulrushes which grew at the side of the Nile, and covered it with a tar-like substance to make it watertight. She put the baby into it and carried it down to the river, where she hid it among the reeds along the bank.

The baby's sister, Miriam, waited a little distance away to see what would happen to her baby brother.

Presently, Pharaoh's daughter came down to the river to bathe, and she suddenly spotted the basket in the reeds. She sent one of her slave-girls to fetch it. When the princess opened it she saw the baby boy. He began to cry and the princess felt sorry for him. 'This is a Hebrew baby,' she said.

Then his sister Miriam had an idea. She ran forward from where she had been hiding and said, 'Shall I go and ask one of the Hebrew women to come and look after him for you?'

'Yes, please do so,' answered Pharaoh's daughter. Miriam hurried off to fetch her own mother.

'Take this baby and look after him for me,' said the princess, 'and I will pay you for doing so.'

The baby's mother was delighted to have her own baby back again.

When the boy was older, she took him again to Pharaoh's daughter, and the princess adopted him as her own son. 'I will call him "Moses".' she said.

So Moses grew up as a prince in Pharaoh's court.

Moses Flees from Egypt

One day when Moses was grown up, he went out to see how his own people, the Hebrews, were living under the hard conditions of the Egyptians.

He was horrified when he saw an Egyptian kill one of the Hebrews. In his anger, Moses killed the Egyptian and buried his body in the sand.

His wicked deed reached the ears of Pharaoh, who thought that Moses deserved to be killed for what he had done. Moses was terrified and fled from the country, and went to live in the land of Midian. When he reached there, he sat down by a well, where the seven daughters of Jethro, the priest of Midian, had come to draw water. Some shepherds tried to drive them away, but Moses went to their rescue.

When they reached home, their father asked how it was that they were back early that day. 'An Egyptian helped us,' they said.

'Why did you leave the man out there?' asked Jethro. 'Go back and invite him to join us for a meal'

So the girls went and brought Moses to their home. He agreed to live with them and helped to take care of Jethro's sheep and goats. After a time, he married one of the daughters.

Many years later the Pharaoh of Egypt died, but the people of Israel were still suffering in their slavery. They asked God to help them and He promised He would send someone to deliver them.

The Burning Bush

One day, when Moses was looking after the flocks of his father-in-law, Jethro, he led them over the desert towards the west, until he came to the holy mountain named Sinai, or Horeb.

While he was there an angel appeared to him as a flame of fire coming from the middle of a bush. Although it was on fire, the bush itself did not seem to be burning up.

'This is strange,' thought Moses. 'I will go nearer and see why this bush is not burnt.'

When he got closer, the voice of God called out, 'Moses! Moses!'

'Do not come any nearer,' said God. 'Take off your shoes, for the place where you are standing is holy ground. I am the God of your ancestors, the God of Abraham, the God of Isaac, and the God of Jacob.'

Moses hid his face, for he was afraid to look at God.

Then God said, 'I know how cruelly My people are suffering in Egypt, and I have heard their prayers to be rescued from the Egyptians. I shall deliver them and bring them out of Egypt to a rich and fertile land. I shall send you to the King of Egypt so that you may rescue the Israelites from his country.'

Moses was appalled at the thought of this tremendous task. He was sure he would not be able to do it, and he thought of one excuse after another, but God had the answer to each of them.

'I am nobody important,' began Moses. 'Who am I to go to Pharaoh? I am not up to such a job.'

God answered, 'But I will be with you.'

'When you have brought the people out,' said God, 'you will worship Me on this mountain.'

'How can I explain who You are?' asked Moses. 'If I say, "The God of your fathers sent me," they will ask, "What is His name?" What shall I say then?'

God replied, 'I am who I am. Tell the people the one who is called "I AM" has sent you, the God of Abraham, Isaac and Jacob. The people will listen to you. But when you ask Pharaoh to let the people go, so that they may offer sacrifices to Me, I know he will not do so unless he is forced. I will use My powers and after that he will let you go.'

'What shall I do if the people don't believe me?' he asked. 'Suppose they say You did not appear before me at all?'

God's answer to this was to give Moses three signs to prove to the people that God had sent him. First He asked Moses to throw the rod he was carrying on to the ground, and when he did so it became a snake. When God told him to pick it up by the tail, it became a staff again.

Next He told Moses to put his hand inside his robe, and when Moses did so his hand was suddenly diseased; but when he put it in and took it out a second time, it was normal and healthy again. Finally God said, 'If they don't believe these two signs, take some water from the River Nile and pour it on the dry ground, and it will turn to blood.'

Moses was still not happy. 'Don't send me, Lord,' he said. 'I am no good at talking. I'm slow and have never been a good speaker.'

God reminded Moses where all powers came from. 'Who is it who gives a man his mouth? Who gives him sight?' He asked. 'It is I, the Lord, and I will help you and tell you what to say.'

'Lord God,' implored Moses, 'please send someone else.'

God replied, 'Your brother Aaron speaks well. In fact, he is on his way to meet you now and will be glad to see you. You can go to Pharaoh together, and you can tell Aaron what to say. I will help you both, and he can be your spokesman. And take your staff with you, for with it you will be able to do great wonders.'

So Moses went back to Jethro, and said, 'Let me go back to my people in Egypt and see if they are still alive.'

Jethro understood and said, 'Go in peace.'

Before Moses left Midian, God reassured him by saying, 'Go back to Egypt, for those who wanted to kill you are now dead.'

Moses set out, and on the way he met his brother. Moses told Aaron all that God had said to him and all the signs and wonders that He had shown him.

Moses and Aaron went off to Egypt, and when they arrived they gathered together all the leaders of the Israelites. Aaron told them all that God had said to Moses, and Moses performed the miracles which God had shown him. The people believed him, and when they heard that God had seen their sufferings under the Egyptians, and that Moses and Aaron had been sent to deliver them, they bowed their heads and worshipped.

The Crossing of the Red Sea

The way from Egypt to Canaan was north east, but it is not absolutely certain which route the Israelites took. It is thought that they did not take the coast road, because there they would have met with Philistine forces, and they were not ready for such an encounter. Instead they began in a generally southerly direction, and at some point crossed the Red Sea, or 'sea of reeds', which may then have extended further north than it does now.

The long procession left Egypt to head for the promised land of which God had told their ancestors and God Himself went in front to show them the way. He appeared as a pillar of cloud during the day and as a pillar of fire during the night; thus they had light and could travel both night and day.

They had not been long on the way when Pharaoh and some of his officials had second thoughts about letting them go. 'Who will now do the work which those slaves did?' they asked. 'Why ever did we let them escape like that?' So Pharaoh decided they must try and bring the Israelites back. He got ready his war chariot and his army and 600 of the best and fastest chariots in the land, and they all chased off after the Israelites.

When the Israelites saw them coming, they were terrified. They were hemmed in by sea and mountains, with the Red Sea in front of them and Pharaoh and his chariots behind them, and they cried out in terror to Moses. 'Did you have to bring us here to die? Aren't there any graves in Egypt? Look what you've done now! We'd have been better staying as slaves to the Egyptians than dying out here in the wilderness.'

'Don't be afraid,' said Moses. 'Just stand firm and you will see what God will do to save you. He will fight for you. There is no need for you to do anything.'

Moses knew that the right thing to do was to trust God, and he wanted the people of Israel to trust Him too.

God said to Moses, 'Tell the people to move forward. Then lift up your rod and hold it over the water; the sea will divide and you may all walk through on dry ground.' Moses agreed to do so.

Then the pillar of cloud moved back until it was between the Israelites and the Egyptians, and so the night passed without the two forces coming near to one another.

The next day Moses held out his rod over the water, and God sent a strong east wind which blew all night and drove the waters back so that they were divided. Then the people were able to walk through on dry land, with water on both sides of them.

Pharaoh's army saw their chance and galloped into the water after them, with all their horses, chariots and horsemen. But their chariots were so heavy that they began to sink in the soft ground, and their wheels became clogged with mud so that they found it difficult to move. The Egyptians said to one another, 'Let's go back out of here, for God is fighting on the side of the Israelites and is against us, the Egyptians.'

'Hold out your hand over the sea,' said God to Moses, 'and the waters will come back over the Egyptians and their chariots and horses.' Moses did so, and by next morning the sea was flowing normally and not one of the Egyptians had reached the other side.

From the far shore the Israelites could see how God had saved them yet again from the Egyptians. There was great rejoicing and the people began to sing in praise of God. Miriam, Moses' and Aaron's sister, and all the other women took up tambourines and danced and sang in praise of God who had delivered them from their enemies.

The Ten Commandments

Under God's guidance, Moses led the people on, away from the Red Sea, and across a great stretch of desert called the Wilderness of Shur. The land was hot, dry and barren, full of sand dunes, scrubland and rocks, and with hardly any water.

'We're hungry,' the people complained. 'At least we had food in Egypt, but now you have brought us out here we shall all starve to death.'

God told Moses, 'I shall send food for you. Each day the people must go out and gather enough for that one day. On the sixth day of the week, they are to gather twice as much as usual.'

That evening a large flock of little brown birds called quail flew into the Israelites' camp; and the people found that they were good to eat.

In the morning, when the dew had gone, the ground was covered with a thin flaky substance, like small white seeds, and as delicate as hoarfrost.

'*Manna*?' asked the Israelites, which means, 'What is it?', and so 'manna' became its name.

Moses said, 'This is the food which God has provided. You are each to gather as much as you need for the day, but no extra.'

The Israelites began gathering, and some gathered more and some less; but it made no difference. Those who had gathered more found that they did not have too much, and those who had gathered little found that there was enough for their needs.

Only on the sixth day of the week could they gather twice as much as usual and then it did not go bad; for the seventh day, the Sabbath, was their day of rest, and they were not to gather food on that day.

God continued to provide manna for the Israelites for the whole of the next forty years until they reached the land of Canaan.

Food was one thing difficult to find in the desert, but, as the Israelites had already discovered, water was another. As they moved on, they again grumbled to Moses that they were thirsty. 'Why do you keep complaining like this?' asked Moses.

Once again the people said, 'Why did you bring us out of Egypt to this miserable place? Must we all die of thirst?' And they grew very angry.

'What can I do with them?' Moses asked God.

'Take some of the leaders and go on ahead of the people,' said God. 'Carry your rod. I will stand before you on a rock on Mount Sinai. Speak to the rock and water will flow out from it.'

Moses went as the Lord had said, but he was so angry with the people that instead of just speaking to the rock, as he had been told, he struck it with his staff. A stream of water flowed out just the same, and the people and animals were able to quench their thirst. But Moses had not obeyed God and so God told him that he would not be the one to lead the people into the promised land.

Moses Receives the Commandments

By now the Israelites had crossed much desert land and had come to the foot of Mount Sinai. From the mountain God called Moses and said, 'Tell the people that I have said these words, "You saw what happened to the Egyptians and how I have brought you safely to this place. Now if you will obey Me and keep My covenant, you will be My chosen people, dedicated to Me alone."'

When the people heard this they replied, 'We will do all that the Lord has said.'

God then told Moses that the people were to make themselves ready for worship and were to put on clean clothes, for He Himself would come down on Mount Sinai. Moses was to put a boundary round the mountain, and the people were not to cross it, or even go near it until they heard a long trumpet blast.

The people made themselves ready as instructed. On the third day there was thunder and lightning and thick cloud on the mountain, which indicated God's power and presence, and a loud blast was heard on a trumpet. All the people trembled with fear. Moses led them to the foot of the mountain, which was wrapped in fire and smoke and shook as if there was an earthquake.

Then God called to Moses alone to go to the top of the mountain; and Moses went up and was lost to view in the cloud. He remained up there for forty days.

While Moses was on the mountain, God gave him the laws by which the Israelites were to live. Among these laws were those which are known as the Ten Commandments, which were written on two tablets of stone by God Himself.

These are the Ten Commandments.
1 *You shall have no other gods before me.*
2 *You shall not make for yourself a graven image, or any likeness of anything that is in heaven above, or that is in the earth beneath or that is in the water under the earth; you shall not bow down to it or serve it.*
3 *You shall not take the name of the Lord your God in vain.*
4 *Remember the sabbath day, to keep it holy. Six days you shall labour, and do all your work; but the seventh day is a day dedicated to the Lord your God; on it no one shall do any work. For in six days the Lord made heaven*

and earth, the sea, and all that is in them, and rested on the seventh day; therefore He blessed the sabbath day and made it holy.

5 *Honour your father and your mother.*

6 *You shall not kill.*

7 *You shall not commit adultery.*

8 *You shall not steal.*

9 *You shall not bear false witness (tell lies) against your neighbour.*

10 *You shall not covet (long to possess) your neighbour's house or wife, or his manservant, or his maidservant, or his ox, or his ass, or anything that belongs to your neighbour.*

The Golden Calf

Moses was away for such a long time that the people grew tired of waiting. They gathered around his brother Aaron and said, 'We don't know what has become of Moses. Let us make a god of our own.'

Aaron, on this occasion, was not firm, and he said to the people. 'Take off the gold earrings which you are wearing, and give them to me.'

They did so, and Aaron took the huge pile of earrings, melted them down, and shaped the gold into a golden calf. Forgetting all about the one true God, the people looked at the golden calf and said, 'This is the god who led us out of Egypt.'

Aaron built an altar before it, and declared that the next day was to be a festival to the Lord. Perhaps he, too, thought it represented the true God, though he should have known better.

Early on the next day, the people brought animals for offerings and they had a great feast.

High up on the mountain God said to Moses, 'You must go down to the people, for they have already forgotten the way I commanded them, and they have made a calf of melted gold and are worshipping it. I am very angry with them.'

As Moses set off back down the mountain, he could hear shouting and noise coming from the people. When he came close enough he saw that they were dancing round the golden calf, and he was so furious that he threw down the tablets and they broke.

He seized the golden calf, melted it and ground what remained to powder. Then he scattered the powder upon the water and made the Israelites drink it as a symbol of their shame and regret.

The next day he went back to God and asked His forgiveness for the sin which the people had committed in worshipping the golden calf. At God's command, he also cut two more tablets of stone, and God gave him the laws again. As a token that they were forgiven, God renewed His promise, or covenant, to the people.

Samuel

In Ramah, not far from Jerusalem, there lived a man named Elkanah. He had two wives, which was not uncommon in those days; one, named Peninnah, had children, but the other, named Hannah, had none.

Each year the whole family went up to the house of the Lord at Shiloh, to offer sacrifices; and each year Hannah felt sadder and sadder because she had no children to take with her. Penninah was not kind about it and used to tease her, so much so that Hannah often wept.

One year Hannah went unhappily into the house of the Lord at Shiloh, and prayed to God that He would send her a son. 'I will dedicate him to You for his whole life,' she said.

Eli, the old priest there, saw her distress and when he went up to her, Hannah told him of her trouble. 'Go in peace,' said Eli, 'and may God answer your prayer.'

God did. In due course Hannah had a fine baby boy, whom she named Samuel. As soon as he was old enough, Hannah fulfilled her promise and took him to the house of the Lord at Shiloh. 'Do you remember me?' she asked Eli. 'This is the child whom God sent to me in answer to my prayer. I have brought him here to dedicate him to the Lord.'

So Samuel became a helper to old Eli, and Eli was very glad of his aid.

Samuel the Prophet

Samuel grew up to be a prophet, a fine man who preached God's word. Not everyone listened, however; there were still many who worshipped idols and refused to obey God's laws.

Then the Philistines went to war with the Israelites and thousands of Israelite men were killed. The Philistines captured the Covenant Box in which were kept the two stone tablets inscribed with the Ten Commandments, and took it away.

The Philistines put the Covenant Box beside their god Dagon, but Dagon fell forward and was smashed to pieces. Then plagues came upon them, and after seven months they wished they had never taken the Covenant Box and decided they had better return it.

How delighted the Israelites were to see the Covenant Box come back.

Samuel knew that Israel would not prosper while they worshipped idols and had no faith in the true God. One day he called the people together and said, 'If you will return to the Lord with all your heart, and serve Him only, then He will rescue you from

the Philistines.' Then Samuel led the people to fast and to confess that they had sinned against God.

Meanwhile, the Philistines were preparing for another battle and, just as Samuel was offering a sacrifice, they came to attack. But God thundered from heaven against them, and they were thrown into a panic. The men of Israel pursued them, and the Philistines were beaten.

Samuel and Saul

One day, when Samuel was an old man, the people went to him and said, 'You are old, and your two sons are not good leaders; therefore will you appoint a king for us.'

Samuel told them all what a king would mean, and how difficult life would be under him. He would take the men for his armies, they and the women would be forced to work and to pay taxes, and they would not have nearly so much freedom as they had now. He would take their best land, and their servants and their best animals too. But the people insisted that they wanted a king. Samuel felt that their only king should be God, and he asked His help.

God had told him that he would send a man whom Samuel was to anoint king of Israel. This man was Saul, the son of a rich man called Kish. Saul was surprised to hear that he had been chosen to be king of the people of Israel.

'But I belong to the smallest tribe in Israel – the tribe of Benjamin,' said Saul, 'and my family is not important.'

But Samuel took a jar of oil and poured it on Saul's head saying, 'The Lord has anointed you to be ruler of his people Israel.' And he gave him certain signs to prove that it was true.

King Saul began his reign well, and although there were some people who did not at first respect him, when they found he was a good leader, they began to obey him. Later on, however, he became self-willed and arrogant, and did not live up to the high hopes which people had of him.

Before long, the Philistines were again assembling to fight the Israelites. They mustered a huge army of war chariots, horsemen and soldiers, and many of the Israelites were terrified and deserted Saul.

Samuel had told Saul to wait seven days for him to come, but Saul thought he knew better and when he saw the people scattering from him, he began to offer a sacrifice without waiting for Samuel. As soon as he had finished, Samuel arrived. He was displeased and told Saul that this disobedience would cost him his kingship, and that God would find another man to replace him.

The battles against the Philistines went on, but Saul did not continue to be a strong king, for he had disobeyed God's commands.

Then God said to Samuel, 'Take some oil and go to Bethlehem, to a man called Jesse, for I have chosen one of his sons to be the next king.'

Samuel did as God had instructed, and when the elders of the town came out to meet him, he invited them to join in the sacrifice.

When he saw Jesse and his family, he particularly noticed his son Eliab, and thought, 'Surely this is the man whom the Lord has chosen.'

But God said to Samuel, 'Do not just look at his appearance or his height, because he is not the man. I, the Lord, do not see as men see. Men look at the outward appearance, but I look at a man's heart.'

Seven of Jesse's sons came out to Samuel, but the Lord did not choose any of them. 'Are all your sons here?' asked Samuel. 'Are there no more?'

'There is only the youngest,' said Jesse, 'but he is out looking after the sheep.'

'Send and fetch him,' said Samuel, 'for we won't start the sacrifice until he comes.'

So Jesse's youngest son, David, was brought in. He was a handsome youth, with beautiful eyes; and God said to Samuel, 'This is the one I have chosen; anoint him.'

Samuel took the horn of oil and anointed David in front of his brothers. God's spirit came to David on that day.

Meanwhile, evil forces had taken charge of Saul, who often became depressed and even violent. His servants thought it might help if he could be soothed with music, so they said, 'Give us the order, sir, and we will find someone who can play the harp. Then when the evil spirit torments you, the musician can play his harp and you will be all right again.' Saul agreed, and asked for a musician to be brought to court.

One of the servants had an idea. 'There is a man named Jesse in Bethlehem,' he said, 'and he has a son who is a good musician.'

'Go and bring him,' Saul ordered.

Messengers went to Jesse, and Jesse sent David to the king's court.

Saul liked David, and whenever he felt tormented by the evil feelings, David was sent for and would bring his harp and play it; and Saul would soon feel better again.

The Wisdom of Solomon

After the death of Saul, David became king. When King David was a very old man, people began to wonder who would succeed him, and so David had his son, Solomon, anointed King.

One night Solomon had a dream in which the Lord God appeared to him and asked, 'What would you like Me to give you now that you are king?'

'I do not know a great deal yet,' said Solomon, 'so give me the wisdom I shall need to rule well, so that I shall be able to tell the difference between good and evil and shall be a fair and just ruler over my people.'

God was pleased and He said to Solomon, 'I will give you a wise and understanding mind, such as no one has had before. Also I will give you gifts for which you have not asked, both riches and honour, so that there will be no other king who can compare with you all your life.

Not long after this, Solomon's new gift of wisdom was put to the test when two women came to him seeking his judgment in a dispute.

One of the women began, 'Your majesty, we are two women both living in the same house and we both gave birth to baby boys within a short time of each other.

'Then one night this woman accidentally lay on her baby and he was smothered and died. While I was still asleep, she took my baby and put her dead baby in my bed.

'No, no,' cried the second woman. 'The living baby is mine and the dead one is yours. You are mistaken.'

And they began to argue in front of the king, for they were very upset.

Solomon said, 'Each of you claims that the living baby is hers and that the dead one belongs to the other woman. Bring me a sword.' A sword was brought to the king and he said, 'Cut the living baby in two and let each mother have half. Then each will have a fair share.'

'No, no!' cried the real mother. 'Let her have the living child, but please don't kill it.' The other mother, however, was quite agreeable to the king's judgment.

Then the king knew which was the real mother – the one who would rather someone else brought up her baby than that it should die. 'Give the living child to the first woman,' he said.

The news of this judgment spread through the land, and all the people were full of respect for Solomon and saw that God had given him great wisdom, so that he would rule justly over them all.

Daniel in the Lions' Den

King Darius, the king of Israel, divided his kingdom into 120 districts, over which he set 120 governors. Then he set Daniel and two other men to be supervisors over the governors.

Although Daniel was an old man, he soon showed that his work was better than that of the other supervisors and governors. Indeed it was so outstanding that the king planned to put him in charge of the whole kingdom.

The other supervisors and governors grew very jealous of Daniel, but he had been a man of God throughout his whole life, and they could never catch him out in anything dishonest or disloyal.

They held a consultation together and said, 'We shall never be able to find anything wrong with Daniel's work; our only hope is to try and catch him out in something connected with the law of his god or with his religion.'

They were well aware that Daniel was in the habit of praying to God three times every day, and they also knew that he had no time for heathen idols and images. So they considered these facts and thought up a crafty plan; then they went to the king with it.

'O king, live for ever,' they said. 'All we governors and officials have agreed that your majesty should issue a new order, and enforce it strictly. It is this: any man who makes any petition to any god or man for the next thirty days, except of course to you, O king, shall be thrown into a den of lions.'

The king was rather flattered at this request from his officials, and he signed the order right away without giving it very much thought. Now, any command written in the king's name and sealed with his ring was held to be unchangeable. When Daniel heard about the new law, he knew what he must do. Never in his life had he been prepared to give up worshipping God, no matter what the cost; now, although he was an old man, he was still prepared to do what he knew to be right, and to face any risk rather than deny God.

He could have given up praying to God for the next thirty days while the law was in force, or he could have gone on praying in secret. But such compromises were not for a man of stern courage such as Daniel, so he ignored the order. He went to his house, where the upstairs windows faced towards Jerusalem and were open, and just as he had always done, he knelt down three times a day and prayed and gave thanks to God.

Now his enemies had him where they wanted him. This was just what they were hoping would happen. They hurried off to the king. 'Your majesty,' they said, 'did you not sign a new order which said that anyone who made any petition to any god or man, other than yourself, for the next thirty days, would be thrown into a den of lions?'

'I did,' said the king.

'But that man Daniel', they went on, 'has disobeyed you. He prays to his god three times every day, just as he did before you made the law.'

The king was very upset when he heard this, for he had a high respect for Daniel, and he realized how he had been trapped by his cunning officials. How he wished he had never signed the new order! The problem continued to worry him all day. He tried very hard to see if there was a way in which Daniel might be rescued from certain death, but always he came up against the problem that an order could not be altered once the king had signed it.

At last, the king concluded that there was no possible way out, and he had to give the order for Daniel to be thrown into the den of lions.

Just before Daniel was taken, the king said to him, 'May your god, whom you serve so faithfully, rescue you.'

Then Daniel was cast into the pit, and a huge stone was brought and placed over the entrance.

Sadly the king returned to the palace where he spent a sleepless night and ate no food. Immediately it became light next morning, he got up and hurried over to the den of lions. He was hoping it might be possible that Daniel was alive – perhaps his god had saved him? But the king thought it far more likely that Daniel would by now have been torn to pieces. It was an agonizing thought.

As soon as he reached the den, he called out anxiously, 'Daniel, servant of the living god, was your god able to save you from the lions?'

To his joy Daniel's voice called back, 'O king, live for ever! My God sent His angel to stop the mouths of the lions, and they have not harmed me at all. God knew that I had not wronged Him or you, your majesty.'

The king was delighted and gave orders that Daniel should immediately be brought up out of the den of lions. When he came out, everyone saw that he was completely unhurt.

King Darius then commanded that the men who had accused Daniel should themselves be thrown into the lions' den, and this was done.

In order to show that he believed Daniel's God to be the true God, King Darius sent out a proclamation saying just this to all peoples, nations and races.